Even though you are a Lioness,
you don't prey on birds.
You enjoy and appreciate them.

Even though you are a crone,
you nevertheless embody
the freshness of a maiden
and the accepting, embracing
love of a mother.

You're a paradox

because you have it all

And you're mysterious
because you accept the mystery.
You let the mystery be.

"Let wonder become familiar,"
said Shakespeare.
You have the gift of 'wonder'.
Therefore you are wonderful.

xo on your birthday, Maggie

Audubon

John James Audubon
Birds of America

Text by
Helgard Reichholf-Riehm

Benedikt Taschen

Front cover:
GREATER FLAMINGO
Phoenicopterus ruber

Illustration page 2:
John Syme: John James Audubon, 1826
Courtesy The White House Collection, Washington D.C.

**This book was printed on 100 % chlorine-free bleached
paper in accordance with the TCF standard.**

© 1994 Benedikt Taschen Verlag GmbH
Hohenzollernring 53, D–50672 Köln
Text: Helgard Reichholf-Riehm, Bad Füssing
Biography: Ingo F. Walther, Alling
Edited by Angelika Muthesius, Cologne
Photographs: Richard Rihm, Munich
Translation: Angela Dunn, Leimen
Composition: Utesch Satztechnik GmbH, Hamburg
Printed by Neue Stalling GmbH & Co KG, Oldenburg

Printed in Germany
ISBN 3-8228-9318-8
GB

AMERI-
CAN
WHITE
PELICAN
Pelecanus
erythro-
rhynchus

6

Audubon's Birds of America

The idea seemed so absurd that no one in the "land of opportunity" was willing to entertain it. On top of it all, the man who presented the idea did not exactly have the best credentials. The illegitimate son of a French captain, he was born on April 26, 1785 in Les Cayes, Haiti. His mother, a French Creole by the name of Jeanne Rabin, died soon after his birth. His father took the boy to Paris, where his "legal mother" brought him up as her own child. Yet at the age of 18 he returned to America, where his father owned property in the Philadelphia area. After a dispute with his father's steward, who regarded the young man as incompetent, Audubon travelled back to France and tried his luck in the French navy – with little success.

By the year 1806, he was back in America again, where he married shortly thereafter and became an American citizen in 1812. A meeting with the foremost American ornithologist of his time, Alexander Wilson, provided the impetus for his plans to publish a comprehensive work on the birds of America, complete with life-size illustrations. Hummingbirds and cardinals presented no difficulty – several of them could be printed on a single page. Even ducks and falcons fit the book's format. But what of herons, flamingos and other large birds? The printers in Philadelphia and New York quite simply believed that the young man was mad. In the meantime he had gone bankrupt and was forced to spend a short time in prison. In 1820 he moved with his family to Cincinnati and later to New Orleans. His wife worked as a governess and he earned a little money here and there, obsessed with the idea of publishing *Birds of America*. It was during this phase that John James Audubon's extrordinary career began.

By the early 1820s he had such an extensive portfolio, mainly watercoloured pencil drawings, that he began to

BALD EAGLE
(White-headed Eagle)
Heliaeetus leucocephalus

7

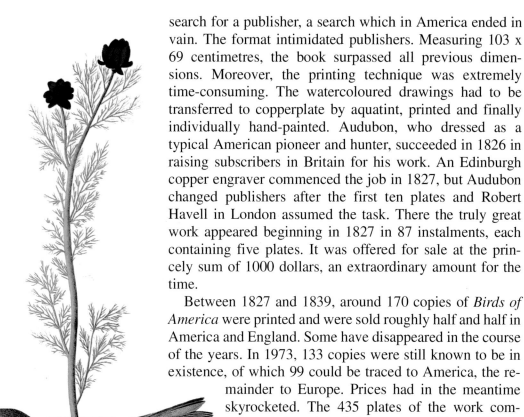

search for a publisher, a search which in America ended in vain. The format intimidated publishers. Measuring 103 x 69 centimetres, the book surpassed all previous dimensions. Moreover, the printing technique was extremely time-consuming. The watercoloured drawings had to be transferred to copperplate by aquatint, printed and finally individually hand-painted. Audubon, who dressed as a typical American pioneer and hunter, succeeded in 1826 in raising subscribers in Britain for his work. An Edinburgh copper engraver commenced the job in 1827, but Audubon changed publishers after the first ten plates and Robert Havell in London assumed the task. There the truly great work appeared beginning in 1827 in 87 instalments, each containing five plates. It was offered for sale at the princely sum of 1000 dollars, an extraordinary amount for the time.

Between 1827 and 1839, around 170 copies of *Birds of America* were printed and were sold roughly half and half in America and England. Some have disappeared in the course of the years. In 1973, 133 copies were still known to be in existence, of which 99 could be traced to America, the remainder to Europe. Prices had in the meantime skyrocketed. The 435 plates of the work commanded a price of almost two million dollars at an auction at Christie's in New York in September 1987. Single plates were sold for between $30,000 and $41,800 – a clear indication of their artistic quality. John James Audubon had raised ornithology illustrations to the level of art. When he died on January 27, 1851, his work represented an almost complete pictorial record of all the bird species of North America. His widow Lucy made the New York Historical Society the recipient of around 400 original watercolours from *Birds of America*, where they can still be admired today. Audubon's idea was not so absurd as it had at first seemed, it had simply gone beyond what was considered possible at the time in America. The British motherland had to adopt the responsibility for the greatest work about the birds of America ever known. The book remains the quintessential work on American birds and Audubon's name lives on in one of the world's most influential

HOODED WARBLER
(Selby's Flycatcher)
Wilsonia citrina

groups of naturalists and conservationists – the Audubon Society.

The man who was "unfit" both for farm work and for military service proved highly adept at lifelike reproductions of natural objects and was an artist of unusual skill. Although he had the opportunity of studying for six months in 1802 under the eminent painter Jacques-Louis David in Paris, the short time was surely only sufficient to grasp new techniques. His mastery was self-taught. This presupposes that Audubon intensively studied the behavioural patterns and movements of the birds he drew. He had to show them in their natural habitat, since only in relation to their habitat do many of the characteristics and peculiarities of the birds make sense. In order to observe the birds in their natural surroundings, Audubon travelled extensively. However, the conditions for travel in those days were restricted by distance as well as time, making it necessary for him to have some species sent to him, which in turn made it difficult for him to classify them. The main problem was size. For many birds even a format of over one metre high and almost three-quarters of a metre wide is too small. It is the way in which Audubon solved this dilemma – even more than the exquisite and carefully detailed paintings of the smaller birds – that has become his hallmark: he simply portrayed the larger birds in positions which fit the book's format. The results were sometimes bizarre and even perplexing. If one was not aware of Audubon's reason for doing this, one might misinterpret it as a lack of drawing technique or as a too rigid reproduction of a model figure.

Extreme examples are the large herons – the great blue heron and the great egret for instance (pp. 21 and p. 18). Audubon illustrated the great blue heron in such a way that the slightly lifted wings and the body fill the upper half of the picture, whereas the neck is curved in a flat arc downwards so that the tips of the open beak point into the lower corner of the picture. The legs are only slightly bent, giving the entire bird a lifelike appearance as it stands at the shore. Even the plumage is displayed, indicating the bird's excitement. Such subtleties underscore the fact that Audubon was

BLACK-THROATED
BLUE WARBLER
Caeruleocantor caerulescens

familiar with the largest of North America's herons from first-hand observations. He wanted nothing more than to depict the birds in the chosen format so that they did not look inanimate. Yet the illustration of the great egret did not quite reach the mark. By placing the bird on a diagonal across the page, thereby showing the plumage of the long body to advantage, Audubon left no space for an aesthetically pleasing portrayal of the long neck. Audubon arranged the corpse of the great egret, which doubtless he used as a model, by bending the neck down towards the breast and stretching the head forward just above the ground.

One thing is certain: the great egret could never strike from this position. Its neck is either stretched straight up or pulled together in a sharp "s" shape, so that the head appears to emerge from between the shoulders. From this "s" position the great egret can strike at lightning speed. The much smaller snowy egret (p. 20) presented no such difficulties of size. This American cousin of the Old World little egret was illustrated by Audubon in a strikingly realistic pose.

The flamingo fell victim to the most extreme of Audubon's space limitations (p. 24). Apparently Audubon never had the chance to observe this species, since even among the small group of flamingos in the background, none is pictured in a posture true to flamingos. The tip of the flamingo's bill has a peculiar boomerang shape and Audubon presented this pointing downwards, apparently because he supposed that the bird would pick in the mud from this position. Moreover, the bird in the background, between the legs of the large bird, is stretching its neck forwards and downwards at an angle. However, flamingos feed in a completely different manner and, had Audubon known this, he would have had no trouble at all depicting the birds with bill and neck in the right position. The flamingo stretches its neck downwards into shallow water, in a straight line or with a slight curve, in such a way that the straight part of the upper bill lies flat on the ground. By moving its lower bill the flamingo pumps water through the sides of the bill. The thick, fleshy tongue acts like a suction pump. The many, fine comb-like slats which surround the edge of the bill filter out water and mud. Crustaceans, mosquito larvae and large algae are thus trapped and swallowed by the flamingos. This form of feeding is only possible with an upper beak which is curved downwards. Despite the fact that flamingos keep their legs straight while feeding, it would have been rel-atively easy for Audubon to capture the birds in their "correct" posture in his sketch book.

Other illustrations, such as that of the smew (p. 32), com-bine a normal stance with an awk-ward one. While the female is seen swimming in a fjord-like bay in a more or less acceptable pose, the magnificent black and white male plummets in exactly the position in which Audubon placed the dead bird on the page. Illustrations of this kind can be found in many other paint-ings. The picture of the white-tailed kite, for example (p. 38), shows the upper bird lying "dead" in the air, while the bird

SURFBIRD
(Townsend's Sandpiper)
Calidris virgata

YELLOW-THROATED
WARBLER
Neodendroica dominica

sitting on the branch appears to be warding off its companion. Audubon was not able to capture the characteristic stationary beating of the wings or perhaps had never seen it first-hand.

By today's standards some of Audubon's dramatic renderings appear exaggerated. Buzzards plunge towards rabbits, carry out battles in the air or clash over prey, while a golden eagle takes flight with a spotless blue hare in its claws (p. 37). Another example is the bald eagle, seen gripping a catfish too large for it. One of the most famous and most prized of the plates shows the white gyrfalcon with black markings (p. 34). Both of the birds featured on this plate are dead and have been painted in the position in which their corpses were arranged. Another snowy-white bird, the extremely rare whooping crane, is pictured in the same "twisted" position as the one Audubon chose for the great egret. The oystercatcher appears set to run a 100-metre race. The common tern plunges from the sky, while the great black-backed gull lifts its right wing as if in the throes of death. Yet none of this diminishes the artistic achievement or the scientific significance of John James Audubon's bird illustrations. Despite the many lifeless poses, Audubon's work in general is distinguished by aesthetic quality and ornithological exactitude. From the countless plates of small birds which could easily be pictured in numbers on the large format, it is clear that Audubon was a fastidious bird-watcher. Considering that they were painted almost two centuries ago, these plates are brimming with characteristic forms of behaviour and expression which are remarkable in their accuracy. Granted, Audubon had to employ a few artist's tricks such as "overdrawing" – the technique of emphasizing conspicuous forms of behaviour. Unlike later artists and ornithologists to whom Audubon's work was available, Audubon himself had no precursors to follow. He had to be content with a rough description of some of the small birds since the spectrum of species of North American birds had not been completely recorded by that time.

Audubon's *Birds of America* are not books for the contemporary ornithologist seeking to practise or perfect bird classification. Audubon's books were replaced by better ones a long time ago, ones which meet the standards expected of bird classification books. The reason why Audubon holds a place of honour amongst American bird lovers and ornithologists is that attitudes towards the bird world began to change earlier than in Europe at a time when America was still young. Although for decades afterwards birds continued to be wiped out, the seeds which had been sown ensured a policy of bird protection that was to be interpreted in a different way from that of Europe. True, burgeoning bird protection came too late to reverse the fate of the now extinct passenger pigeon or Carolina parakeet. Even the massive decimation of white herons in the colonies could not be prevented. They sacrificed their feathers – and lives – for the greater good of the millinery trade. The underlying difference is one of attitude. The earlier nature and bird conservationists considered the "thieving and murdering" eagles, falcons, hawks and buzzards as much a part of the repertoire of the natural beauty of the American wilderness as the "fishing" herons, pelicans and cormorants. Birds were not separated into "good" and "evil", the former being songbirds which eliminated insects and for whom nesting boxes were built and the latter being those which caused damage to game and fish which could otherwise be hunted. Although bird conservationists in Europe do not like to be reminded of the fact, this attitude still persists today. It has led to an unfortunate, ongoing, decades-old dispute not only between hunters and fishermen on the one hand and

COMMON MOORHEN
Gallinula chloropus

bird conservationists on the other, but also within the bird protection community itself.

In Europe one cannot imagine what is taken for granted in America: ospreys build their aeries in yachting marinas and catch fish between the fishing boots; fishermen separate the good fish from their catch and feed pelicans and cormorants or herons with the leftovers. Buzzards and eagles do not flee hundreds of metres as soon as they spot a human being, while visitors may enter the nesting grounds of the most rare water birds without disturbing them. We are not talking about remote islands, but about regions near the major cities in Florida, about the east coast and the coast of California, accessible to millions of people. Nor are we talking of exotic species to be found only in the wilds of America, but of birds whose related species are found in Europe, where they are considerably more distrustful of homo sapiens.

It goes without saying that Americans feed songbirds in winter and build bird houses for them. They enjoy swallows and the songs of some species, are pleased with the trusting nature of hummingbirds, and donate sums of money to bird protection agencies. But what distinguishes them from Europeans is their tolerance towards all species of birds which supposedly or actually are responsible for damage to crops, to game or fish, which might otherwise be hunted. Given this attitude, it is no wonder that a book such as Rachel Carson's *Silent Spring* could cause such a furore. It was not the fear of a drop in numbers of "acceptable" songbirds which led to a swift ban on DDT in the United States. Rather, it was the devastation which this environmental poison had brought about amongst eagles and pelicans, herons and other large birds – the very birds which hunters and fishermen in Europe often claim should be held in check. The seeds which Audubon sowed had produced fruit. American birds had not been divided into "good" and "evil" in the antiquated, European way. Each species is and remains important and worthy of preserving, regardless of whether it be the bald eagle of the American crest or an ordinary finch or a small owl known only to a handful of knowledgeable ornithologists. The Audubon Society, named after John James Audubon, early on established conservation areas where the birds thrived. The wildlife reserves of this private nature protection agency surpass even the excellent state-funded national park and reserve system. In contrast to conservation areas in Europe which exist only on paper, the American conservation regions are very real. Specially trained rangers look after the reserves and ensure that no damage is caused by the many tourists who visit each year. For many visitors, the experience of coming into close contact with nature is rewarding because they are made aware of the beauty and exceptional features of the conservation area. Anyone seeing a heron snatch a shrimp and fly to a dock to break the shrimp open with its bill, in spite of the presence of astonished onlookers, is likely to look at herons with different eyes from then on. What a different attitude such people have from those who read how herons and cormorants kill off the stock of fish in our lakes. Whereas visitors to European conservation areas are either not permitted entry or forced to remain on footpaths, those exploiting nature are allowed to continue working unhampered almost without exception. This usually leads to bitter protest rather than welcoming cheers at the announcement of a nature conservation area. From the beginning, the Americans took the opposite approach. Conservation areas were not to be "used", a notion which runs counter to the purpose of protection. Instead the parks were opened to the nature-loving public. America has reason to be proud of its conservation areas which, unlike those in central Europe,

BARN SWALLOW
Hirundo rustica

fulfil the purpose they were designed to serve. Audubon's spirit pervades American nature protection, even though he often collected the models for his illustrations with a shotgun. Nature protection and hunting were never incompatible since, on principle, even the species which could be hunted belonged to everyone and were not considered the private property of a single person. For this reason, hunters and nature conservationists could establish a nature conservation system which has prospered and which has long since achieved what is still only a dream in Europe. For example, the stock of waterfowl is kept at a certain level and sportsmen are given the chance to hunt the surplus each year.

In effect, it may be said that the American spirit is the reason that so much more has been achieved in the field of nature and bird conservation than in Europe, particularly central Europe. John James Audubon's work played a crucial role in shaping this "American spirit", which lives on in his life work, a work unmatched in its artistic and historical significance. We have to envy America for this attitude of mind and the success which has sprung from it.

NORTHERN
PARULA
WARBLER
(Blue Yellow-back
Warbler)
Parula americana

16

I

DIVERS OF LAKES AND BAYS,
WANDERERS OF SEAS AND COASTS

Page 17

LIGHT-MANTLED SOOTY
ALBATROSS
(Dusky Albatross)
Phoebetria palpebrata

GREAT EGRET
Casmerodius albus

Although distributed across the
world, this large snowy-white egret
is nowhere to be found in numbers.
Its main feature is the splendour of
its white plumage. The great egret's
habitat is large lagoons with reedy
shores and shallow inland lakes,
where it feeds primarily on fish.
The birds perform a highly im-
pressive mating display.

RED-NECKED GREBE
Podiceps grisegena

The red-necked grebe is one of the
lobe-toed diving birds with folds of
skin on the toes rather than webbed
feet. Agile under water, grebes are
quite clumsy on land. When diving,
the wings are kept in pouches
where the young can also be hid-
den. Even when underwater, the
young remain protected in these
pouches.

Page 20

SNOWY EGRET
(Snowy Heron)
Egretta thula

Page 21

GREAT BLUE HERON
Ardea herodias

20

21

SCARLET IBIS
Eudocimus ruber

The deep red colour of the scarlet ibis results from its food, which consists of dark red worms. The dye contained in the worms is similar to the haemoglobin of human blood. The scarlet ibis breeds in colonies in the mangrove swamps in northern South America. They hunt for food in groups in the brackish water of lagoons.

REDDISH EGRET
(Purple Heron)
Dichromonassa rufescens

The reddish egret can be identified most readily by the two colours of its bill. Otherwise it is similar in its dark phase to the blue heron and to the great egret during its white phase. Dark versions appear more often in the western area of this bird's range, which extends to the Gulf of Mexico. Mixed pairs, particularly appealing to bird-watchers, can be sighted annually.

During the winter months the reddish egret migrates to central America.

Page 24

GREATER FLAMINGO
Phoenicopterus ruber

The observer is always astounded at the manner in which flamingos procure their food. The flamingo twists its head down so that the upper bill faces downwards and the lower bill upwards. With rhythmic pumping movements of its thick tongue, the flamingo strains food from the water.

II

WATERFOWL

MALLARD
(Mallard Duck)
Anas platyrhynchos

WHISTLING SWAN
Olor columbianus

Despite its name, the most common
swan in North America does not
whistle. Its hissing calls to mind
the cry of a European relative, the
mute swan. The North American
tundra is breeding ground for whistling swans, which spend the winter
in the south. In Chesapeake Bay
they have even become a tourist at-
traction.

TRUMPETER SWAN

Olor buccinator

The sonorous call of the trumpeter swan should not be missed by any nature lover. Yet in the 1930s these wonderful birds were nearly extinct. Measures to protect the bird were introduced in time to see the numbers significantly increase again. Unlike the melodies of songbirds which come from the syrinx, the trumpeter swan produces its cry with the windpipe of its unusually long neck.

Page 29

WOOD DUCK

Aix sponsa

The handsome wood duck is the adornment of many park ponds. Their habitat is the wooded lakes and streams of North America. The female lays eight to ten eggs in an abandoned tree cavity where the eggs are hatched. Shortly after hatching, the chicks jump out of their nest and do not appear to be bothered if they hit the ground rather than the water.

29

LABRADOR DUCK

Camptorhynchus labradorius

Audubon had the good luck to see this rare duck which became extinct in the mid-19th century. Experts however, never had the chance to observe the labrador duck in its nesting terrain in Labrador. The ducks were hunted on their wintering grounds on the Atlantic coast of North America. The meat of the ducks was of little value, a fact which underscores the tragedy of the labrador's extinction.

GOOSANDER

(Common Merganser)
Mergus merganser

Goosanders are a type of water-fowl. They breed on many of the freshwater lakes and rivers of Europe and North America where they skillfully hunt fish under water. Goosanders are able to grip fish in their bills, which are lined with small pointed teeth. Many goosanders have had to pay with their lives for their love of fish, since fishermen consider them as competition.

Page 32

SMEW

(White Nun)
Mergus albellus

Few people are familiar with this small, pretty, black and white water-fowl, which is distributed widely across northern Europe and North America. It breeds on freshwater lakes and rivers, where it subsists on small fish and other water creatures. The birds migrate south for the winter, making stopovers at reservoirs and even on urban waters.

SCAVENGERS AND BIRDS OF PREY

HARRIS' HAWK
(Bay-winged Hawk)
Parabuteo unicinctus

GYRFALCON
(Iceland or Jer Falcon)
Hierofalco rusticolus

Snowy-white gyrfalcons, still highly prized by falconers, thrill observers with their enthusiasm for the chase and their speed. Gyrfalcons live in the Arctic tundra of North America and Eurasia, but are nowhere to be found in numbers. The white feathers act as a natural camouflage in the open, snow-covered landscape, where the gyrfalcon cannot hide as it hunts for prey. Gyrfalcons hunt white grouse and ducks.

CALIFORNIA CONDOR
(Californian Vulture)
Gymnogyps californianus

With a wingspan of almost three metres, this relative of the Andean condor is currently the subject of a campaign to protect it from extinction. Condors were taken into captivity to be bred in zoos after it became obvious that they could not survive in their native habitat. Success has been reported in releasing birds born in captivity back to nature.

OSPREY
Pandion haliaetus

This highly-specialized hawk lives exclusively on fish which it catches by plunging into the water, sometimes disappearing underwater and grasping the slippery catch in its claws. The numbers of this bird which is found on all continents have been drastically diminished by environmental pollution and persecution. Where it is not hunted, the osprey accustoms itself to humans and has even been known to build nests in yachting marinas.

Page 37

GOLDEN EAGLE
Aquila chrysaetos

Archetype of the eagle and standard for many a coat of arms, the golden eagle is widespread in North America and Europe. Although it has a wingspan of over two metres, it can only carry small prey, roughly the size of a blue hare.

Page 38

WHITE-TAILED KITE
Elanus caeruleus

For a long time the American Everglades were considered the last retreat in North America for the black-shouldered kite. That is, until it found a new place to live – golf courses. For some golf clubs this bird has become a symbol, and it is impossible to imagine them without a black-shouldered kite. The bird is found as far away as in the southern parts of South America.

38

IV

UPLAND GAMEBIRDS
AND MARSH-DWELLERS

KING RAIL

(Fresh-water Marsh Hen)
Rallus elegans

SANDHILL CRANE
Grus canadensis

Every year, thousands of sandhill cranes fly south with loud, melodic calls, from the Arctic tundra to the Mississippi delta and on to Florida. They fly in the typical V-formation at a height of some 400 metres. They lay their eggs on swampy ground, well-protected from enemies, where they can raise their young. Only two eggs are laid and each parent assumes responsibility for one of the young after they have been hatched.

Page 41

WHOOPING CRANE
Grus americana

Only fifteen whooping cranes remained in the wilds in 1941–42. Under intensive protective measures their numbers have risen to over 200, but the whooping crane remains one of the most endangered bird species in the world. Their only breeding ground is the Wood Buffalo National Park in Canada.

41

ROCK PTARMIGAN
(Rock Grouse)
Lagopus mutus

Roughly the size of a partridge, the
rock ptarmigan is found across the
higher altitudes of North America
and Eurasia. In winter they are almost pure white, in autumn and
spring speckled, while in summer
their feathers are brown. In this
way they blend into their environment according to the season.

RUFFED GROUSE
Bonasa umbellus

People have long been fascinated by the mating display and appearance of the ruffed grouse. Highly coveted as game and as trophies, the birds have been mercilessly hunted. As a home, the ruffed grouse prefers the poplar and birch woods of Canada and the northern United States.

Page 44

CLAPPER RAIL
(Salt-water Marsh Hen)
Rallus longirostris

Although closely related to the king rail, the clapper rail differs from its cousin in its choice of habitat. Whereas the clapper rail nests in salt marshes near the coast, the king rail is partial to fresh-water swamps.

44

V

SHOREBIRDS

Page 45

BLACK-NECKED STILT

(Long-legged Avocet)
Himantopus mexicanus

MARBLED GODWIT

(Great Marbled Godwit)
Limosa fedoa

The marbled godwit breeds in the marshy areas of the Canadian prairie provinces along the many small lakes left behind by glaciers 8000 years ago. Its marbled and flecked feathers have lent this bird of the plover family its name.

Page 47

WHIMBREL

(Great Esquimaux Curlew)
Numenius phaeopus

In Europe the slightly larger curlews are better known, but the whimbrel has a wider range. Breeding in North America and Eurasia, the birds travel south to the tropics for the winter months. Although it is possible to overlook the whimbrel due to its colouring, one would be unlikely to mistake its call. Indeed, the name whimbrel is derived from its melodious warbling.

AMERICAN AVOCET
Recurvirostra americana

Its brown neck distinguishes the American avocet from the closely-related European avocet. However, the two types are identical in their behaviour and way of life. With a sweeping motion avocets drag their upturned bills back and forth through the water in their quest for small fish and water insects.

BLACK OYSTERCATCHER
(Bachman's or White-legged Oystercatcher)
Haematopus bachmani

BLACKISH OYSTER-CATCHER
(Slender-billed or Townsend's Oystercatcher)
Haematopus ater

This sombre coloured relative of the European oystercatcher lives on the west coast of America. The black oystercatcher's habitat is the dark, cliff-lined coast of North America. Like its southern cousin, the blackish oystercatcher, it feeds on worms, snails and mussels which it prises off the rocks with its powerful bill.

Page 50

GREENSHANK
Tringa nebularia

Oddly enough, Audubon drew the greenshank which is native to Eurasia but not to North America. The greenshank's North American counterpart is the yellowlegs. Both species were named for the colour of their long legs. These waders search for food in the soft mud of shallow waters.

50

VI

SEABIRDS

Page 51

RING-BILLED GULL
(Common Gull)
Larus delawarensis

GLAUCOUS GULL
(Burgomaster Gull)
Larus hyperboreus

The glaucous gull is one of the few birds which has an almost completely white plumage. Even the tips of its wings are white, unlike other gulls, whose wingtips are black. The glaucous gull is a large, powerful bird which is found in the North Atlantic where it preys on young or weak auks and other seabirds – even gulls. However, it also includes carrion and trash in its diet.

GREAT AUK

Pinguinus impennis

This bird, unable to fly and now extinct, could be located until well
into the 18th century in its breeding
grounds on the islands of the North
Atlantic. In 1844, when Audubon
was still alive, the last pair was
slaughtered and its eggs destroyed.
As with the penguins of the southern oceans, the great auk's wings
were adapted to be used as paddles.

BLACK GUILLEMOT
Cepphus grylle

The guillemot uses its mighty
wings and feet in its quest for fish.
Like the 21 relatives of the family
of auks, its habitat covers an area
stretching from the North Atlantic
to the Arctic Ocean. It lays its eggs
in rocky recesses, often at considerable and quite inaccessible heights.
Unlike other auks, it does not form
large colonies. For these reasons it
has been relatively protected from
humans.

Page 55

COMMON TERN
(*Great Tern*)
Sterna hirundo

The elegant great tern lives on the
lakes and rivers of North America's
prairies, similar to its habitat in Europe's interior. As in Europe, the female leaves the nest shortly after
brooding over the young and flies
with them to the sea. There they
spend the greater part of their lives,
migrating repeatedly up and down
the coast as far south as the tropical
southern Atlantic.

HORNED PUFFIN
(Large-billed Puffin)
Fratercula corniculata

The horned puffin, closely related
to the European puffin, got its
name from its horn-like "eyebrow".
The combination of eyebrows and
an imposing bill result in an amus-
ing appearance which is heightened
when several eels are seen hanging
out of the bill. These puffins breed
around the Bering Sea. After the
mating season the intensive colour
fades and the horny eyebrow atro-
phies.

Page 58

GREATER BLACK-
BACKED GULL
Larus marinus

This gull is one of the largest in the
world. It grows to a height of almost 70 centimetres and reaches a
wingspan of 160 centimetres. Such
a large bird naturally needs great
quantities of food, which it finds
near coasts and in trash heaps. Its
range extends from the British Isles
to Spitzbergen, across to the south
of Greenland and the west coast of
North America.

VII

SHOWY BIRDS, NOCTURNAL HUNTERS AND SUPERB AERIALISTS

60

SAW-WHET OWL

Aegolius acadicus

WHITE-CROWNED PIGEON

Patagioenas leucocephala

Although actually at home in the western Antilles, this medium-sized pigeon also breeds in the mangrove swamps of the Florida Keys. Neither timid nor rare, this bird can actually be sighted from the roads leading to the Florida Keys. Quite unlike most pigeons, white-crowned pigeons breed in colonies in the thick underbrush of the mangroves.

PASSENGER PIGEON

Ectopistes migratoria

It is unfathomable how a species of bird whose flocks a hundred years ago numbered millions could die out. So plentiful were passenger pigeons that the sky was plunged into darkness when they passed over. The largest flock ever was estimated to be some two billion strong. The last passenger pigeon died in 1914 in Cincinnati Zoo.

YELLOW-BILLED CUCKOO

Coccyzus americanus

In Europe the cuckoo represents brood parasitism, although the same is not true of non-European cuckoos. The yellow-billed cuckoo, for instance, usually builds itself a nest and brings up its own young. However, there are regular incidents of it foisting its eggs on the black-billed cuckoo. Its food consists mainly of hairy caterpillars and other insects.

Page 63

RUBY-THROATED HUMMING-BIRD

Archilocus colubris

Who is not impressed by the flying skills of the humming-bird and who does not admire its brilliant colours? Its range stretches from Canada to Argentina, from the lowlands of the Amazon to the heights of the Andes. Despite its tiny size, the ruby-throated humming-bird crosses the Gulf of Mexico non-stop. It requires a mere two grammes of body fat for this flight!

Page 64

CAROLINA PARAKEET

Conuropsis carolinensis

The Carolina parakeet was the only parakeet in North America and still quite common in Audubon's time. However, owing to its handsome plumage and even more to its predilection for fruit and corn, the parakeet was killed off in numbers and eventually rendered extinct. As with most types of parakeets, the Carolina lived and bred in large colonies. The last of its kind died in 1914 in Cincinnati Zoo.

63

GREAT HORNED OWL
Bubo virginianus

The largest and most powerful of the American owls is the great horned owl. It is almost the same size as its European cousin, the eagle-owl (Bubo bubo).

MANGROVE CUCKOO
Coccyzus minor

The mangrove cuckoo, roughly 30cm in length, leads a secluded life in the black and white mangrove areas in Florida, from which it got its name. Even though it is a true cuckoo, it builds its own nest and raises its own young. Its distinguishing feature is the long black and white tail.

Page 67

GREAT GRAY OWL
(Great Cinereous Owl)
Strix nebulosa

Nearly as large as the eagle owl, the great gray owl's habitat covers the northern coniferous forests of Eurasia and North America. It is protected from the cold by its soft feathers, which lend it a rotund appearance. Silently, with no sound of flapping wings, it soars through the forests. It lives chiefly on small mammals. The great gray owl's "beard" makes its face so expressive.

Page 68

COMMON NIGHTHAWK
(Night Hawk)
Chordeiles minor

Widely distributed across America, the night hawk resembles in appearance and way of life the European night hawk. The size of a cuckoo, this hawk is not visible on the ground, due to its colouring.

68

VIII

GLEANERS OF FOREST AND MEADOW

Page 69

BLACK-BILLED MAGPIE
(American Magpie)
Pica pica

Page 70

BELTED KINGFISHER
Streptoceryle alcyon

At a length of 33cm, this kingfisher is considerably larger than its
European cousin. Larger, too, are
the fish which it catches. The
belted kingfisher enjoys distribution across the whole of North
America and can be observed near
a variety of waters.

BLACK-BACKED THREE-TOED WOODPECKER
Picoides arcticus

This woodpecker is a distinctive
bird of the northern Canadian
forests. It is similar to the European
three-toed woodpecker. Gripping
the bark with its flat toes, the woodpecker can climb with agility.

FORK-TAILED FLYCATCHER
Tyrannus savana

It is seldom that one has the chance to observe the fork-tailed flycatcher in the southern states of America. Its actual habitat is the tropics of central and South America, where the flycatcher is quite common and easily sighted on the open savannas where it lives.

Page 73

TREE SWALLOW
(White-bellied Swallow or Green-blue Swallow)
Tachycineta bicolor

In German the tree swallow is known as the "marsh swallow". Both the English and the German names are fitting, since this pretty two-coloured swallow inhabits swampy woods where it nests in abandoned woodpecker holes. Its breeding ground reaches as far as Alaska, although it migrates south in autumn.

Page 74

MAGPIE JAY
(Columbia Jay)
Calocitta formosa

This breathtaking bird, a relative of the crows and jays of Europe, is found chiefly in Mexico. However, it is occasionally sighted in southern America. It lives in the sparsely wooded parts of forests of the mountains which drop away to the Pacific. Little is known about its habits. A distinguishing feature is the long tail, not unlike that of the magpie.

IX

SONGSTERS AND MIMICS

EASTERN BLUEBIRD

Sialia sialis

VEERY

(Tawny Thrush)

Catharus fuscescens

Originally this attractive, sparingly
dotted thrush was common and
widespread throughout North
America. Numbers decreased due
to changes in land use. The veery
can be found in damp mixed forests
where it retreats into the underbrush.

VARIED THRUSH

Ixoreus naevius

SAGE THRASHER

(Mountain Mocking Bird)

Toxastoma montanum

These two types of thrush are native to both Eurasia and North
America. They resemble each other
in appearance, breeding habits as
well as in their choice of food and
habitat. Most species are light to
medium brown, spotted and
roughly the size of a blackbird.
They spend the majority of their
time on the ground. Unlike the varied thrush, which it the most colour-
ful of all thrushes native to
America, the sage thrasher has the
typical characteristics of its family.

BOHEMIAN WAXWING
Bombycilla garrulus

This appealing bird is better known to bird lovers in Europe than to those in America since it makes its home in the remote northern coniferous forests. Another, similar species, the somewhat smaller cedar waxwing is also found in America. The waxwings visit, or rather invade, central Europe more or less regularly in winter. They tarry on berry branches in gardens and parks.

CUVIER'S KINGLET
Regulus cuvieri

Weighing in at just five grammes, the cuvier's kinglet is one of the smallest birds in the world. Owing to its preference for the treetops, it is often overlooked. Yet it enjoys a wide range in North America and Eurasia and is plentiful everywhere. Like the titmouse, it is a convivial creature. Only during the period of incubation does it defend its small territory.

TOWNSEND'S WARBLER
Dendroica townsendi

MOUNTAIN BLUEBIRD
(Arctic Bluebird)
Sialia currucoides

WESTERN BLUEBIRD
Sialia mexicana

X

WOODLAND SPRITES

Page 81
YELLOW-BREASTED CHAT
Icteria virens

YELLOW-THROATED
VIREO
Vireo flavifrons

The small yellow-throated vireo is considered to be the prettiest of its family and like songbirds, tanagers and shrikes, favours park-like country. Vireos build elaborate nests from fine grasses, spider webs and mosses and hang them from a fork in the branch of a tree, well-protected from enemies. Originally the yellow-throated vireo was more common and had an appreciably wider range.

Page 83
WARBLING VIREO
(Warbling Flycatcher)
Vireosylva gilva

Its appearance is deceptive: although the look and habits of the warbling vireo recall the Old World warblers, it is in fact a true leaf shrike. The dainty nest, hung from a forked branch, the shape of the beak and the slow movements leave no doubt as to its relatives. The warbling vireo is found in the open wooded countryside of North America but winters in central America.

83

YELLOW WARBLER
(Rathbone Warbler)
Dendroica petechia

The yellow warbler is the most widespread of all the American warblers, with nesting grounds stretching from Canada to the Galapagos Islands. An inhabitant of sparsely-wooded forests, it also enjoys copses and gardens. Its pretty yellow feathers, delicate voice and ubiquity combine to make the yellow warbler one of the best known and best loved of the North American songbirds.

CONNECTICUT WARBLER
Oporornis agilis

This timid and rarely sighted warbler can be identified by the white ring around its eyes. Contrary to its name, the Connecticut warbler only passes through this American state in the autumn. Its breeding grounds extend from southern and central Canada to northern Michigan.

Page 86

AMERICAN REDSTART
Setophaga ruticilla

The American redstart lifts its wings in its courtship display just as the flycatchers do. The orange spot of the males and the yellow marking of the females light up against the otherwise black feathers. Their distribution extends from Alaska over Canada and into the United States, where the species is one of the most widespread and popular of the warblers.

XI

FLOCKERS AND SONGBIRDS

CARDINAL COMMON
Cardinalis cardinalis

SEASIDE SPARROW
(MacGillivray's Finch)
Ammospiza maritima

This plain, shy sparrow is rarely observed. It lives in the brackish swamps between Massachusetts and Texas where, in loose colonies, it nests in the heavy underbrush. The seaside sparrow has adapted to this environment by developing large claws with which it can skip over the mud without sinking in. It looks for food on the mud flats.

PURPLE GRACKLE
Quiscalus quiscula

Slightly larger than the blackbird, the lively purple grackle is easily recognized by its lack of timidity, its bright yellow eyes and the iridescent shine of its bronze and violet plumage. Moreover, it is a sociable bird which enjoys exercising its voice. Using its sturdy beak, the grackle pokes the ground looking for insects and worms – just as the starling does. Its range includes almost the entire North American continent, east of the Rocky Mountains.

89

90

WHITE-WINGED CROSS-BILL

Loxia leucoptera

Watching this bird picking at a pine cone with its powerful crossed beak, one might well assume it was a parrot. It is easy to distinguish from the red crossbill (which lives further south) by the white bands on its shoulders. The white-winged crossbill has been known to invade the south. Otherwise it keeps to its nesting grounds in Canada and Alaska.

DICKCISSEL

(Black-throated Bunting)
Spiza americana

This little finch was named for the sound of its call – "dick-dick-dick-cissel". In spring this tune is heard from many fences and power lines. Now and again flocks of dickcissel invade fields of lucerne in the grass-lands of the American midwest.

WHITE-CROWNED SPARROW
Zonotrichia leucophrys

This handsome little bunting is widespread on the American continent. White-crowned sparrows are social creatures. On the ground they search for seeds, fruits and insects. However, they are unwelcome guests in gardens where they peck at seedlings. The white-crowned sparrow builds its nest in low, dense bushes.

Page 93

NORTHERN ORIOLE
(Baltimore Oriole)
Icterus galbula

Audubon was fascinated by the yellowish-orange and black plumage of the Baltimore oriole, which shines so brightly during courting rituals. The colours are intensified by the beating of the wings. A very striking bird, it ranges across almost the entire North American continent. Similar oriole species are to be found in places where the Baltimore is not. Its song resembles that of the starling.

John James Audubon: Life and Work

John James Audubon (1785–1851) was born on **April 26, 1785** in Les Cayes on the island of Santo Domingo (today Haiti, in former times Hispaniola) in the West Indies. He was the illegitimate son of Jean Audubon, a French naval captain and agent of a French trading company situated in Nantes. Audubon's mother, Jeanne Rabin, was a French woman of Creole descent who died not long after his birth. This unusual background fostered wild rumours which Audubon apparently encouraged. As a consequence, some believed him to be the missing son of Louis XVI, the dauphin, who died or disappeared in 1795. Accompanied by his father, Audubon travelled to Paris in **1789** where he lived with his legal mother, who accepted and raised him as her own child. At this time, he began to observe and draw birds. In **1802** he took drawing lessons for six months with the famous painter Jacques-Louis David. At the age of 18, in **1803**, Audubon returned to America where his father owned land near Philadelphia. He studied nature and drew steadily, especially birds. After an argument with the steward of his father's estate, who considered him unsuitable for any kind of practical work, Audubon returned to France where he served for a short time in the French navy. However, in **1806** he travelled back to America again and worked in the haberdashery trade in Kentucky. In **1808** he married Lucy Bakewell, a neighbour's daughter. Shortly thereafter, he met Alexander Wilson, the leading American ornithologist of the time, who also had plans for a great work about the birds of America. Audubon became an American citizen in **1812**. The end of his career as a businessman came in **1819**, when he spent a short time in debtor's prison due to bankruptcy. In **1820** he moved with the family to Cincinnati and later to New Orleans where he eked out a living as a dancing and fencing teacher and as a portraitist, while his wife worked as a governess. By this time he had collected several pieces, mostly watercoloured pencil drawings, for a book with plates to be called *Birds of America*. Unable to find either a satisfactory printer or publisher in Philadelphia or New York, Audubon travelled to England and Scotland in **1826**, where he had more success and even found subscribers for his work. William Lizars, a copperplate engraver, began printing in Edinburgh in **1827**. Audubon insisted on life-size reproductions of the birds. Where this was not possible – for example, with the great blue heron or the flamingo – he depicted them with the neck stretching downwards. Nevertheless, the oversized format of the book (103 x 69 cm), then the largest known book format, created problems. Audubon's watercoloured drawings were first transferred to copperplates by means of the aquatint technique, then printed and individually painted by hand. After the first ten plates had been finished, Audubon changed printers and went to Robert Havell in London. The work was published in 87 instalments beginning in **1827**, each instalment consisting of five plates, and each selling for the considerable price of 1,000 dollars. Audubon returned to America in **1829**. An expedition in **1834** took him to Texas, Florida, Labrador and along the Mississippi as well as to other destinations. During this time he completed his drawings. In **1841** he moved to Manhattan. On **January 27, 1851**, Audubon passed away after returning from a trip to Europe.

LONG-EARED OWL
Asio otus

In **1863**, Audubon's widow Lucy sold around four hundred original watercolours of the *Birds of America* to the New York Historical Society, where they remain to this day. Although today some of his depictions are criticized as ornithologically imprecise or exaggeratedly dramatic, Audubon's significance lies in the fact that, despite the modest means and tools of his day, he raised his zoological illustrations to the level of works of art.

Between 1827 and 1839 Audubon had approximately 170 copies of *Birds of America* printed. Of them, 82 were sold in America and 79 in England. By 1973, 133 copies could still be traced, 99 to America and 34 in Europe. Since that time, 13 copies have been sold, 11 of them as single plates. At the last auction of a copy at Christie's in New York on September 14–15, 1987 a record price of $1,930,000 was paid for the 435 plates. The highest prices were commanded by the two swans, the great blue heron and the flamingo at $41,800 each, the snowy egret at $33,000 and the whooping crane and gyrfalcon at $30,800 each.

Ingo F. Walther

Bibliography

Own Writings
The Birds of America, 4 Vols., London 1827–1839
("Double Elephant Folio").
Ornithological Biography, 5 Vols., Edinburgh 1831–1839 (accompanying text).
A Synopsis of the Birds of America, London and Edinburgh 1839.
The Birds of America, 7 Vols., New York and Philadelphia 1840–1842 (octavo).
The Viviparous Quadrupeds of North America, 2 Vols., New York 1845–1848.
Literature on Audubon
L. Audubon: The Life of John James Audubon, the Naturalist, New York 1869.
M. R. Audubon: Audubon and his Journals, 2 Vols., London 1898.
F. H. Herrick: Audubon, the Naturalist, 2 Vols., New York 1917.
S. C. Arthur: Audubon, New Orleans 1937.
W. Vogt: The Birds of America by J.J. Audubon, New York 1937.
D. C. Peattie: Audubon's America, Boston 1940.
C. Rourke: Audubon, New York 1947.
G. C. Fisher: Life of Audubon, 1949.
W. H. Fries: The Double Elephant Folio: The Story of Audubon's Birds of America, Chicago 1973.
T. Clark and L. E. Bannon: Handbook of Audubon Prints, Gretna (LA) 1980.
R. T. Peterson and V. M. Peterson (Eds.): The Audubon Society Baby Elephant Folio. Audubon's
Birds of America, New York 1981.